SONGS TO THE BELOVED
AND HER LOVERS

Other books in the Songs of Love series,
written by Nicholas Michael Morrow and
illustrated by Willow Arlenea:

Book 2 ~ *Songs to the Beloved in Gratitude and Praise*
Book 3 ~ *Sea of Compassion: Songs of Becoming*
Book 4 ~ *Gowns of Glory: Songs of Awakening*
Book 5 ~ *Nymph Sutra: Songs of Fire*
Book 6 ~ *Elfin Chronicle: Songs of Enchantment*
Book 7 ~ *Earth Saga: Songs of Entonement*
Book 8 ~ *Mountain Oracle: Songs of Initiation*
Book 9 ~ *Encounters with the Beloved: Songs of Oneness*

SONGS TO THE BELOVED AND HER LOVERS

Nicholas Michael Morrow

Illustrations by Willow Arlenea

GAIA GROVE
PUBLISHING

Ranchos de Taos, New Mexico

Published by:
Gaia Grove Publishing
PO Box 2888, Ranchos de Taos, NM 87557
gaiagrovepublishing.com

Gaia Grove Publishing is dedicated to the publication and performance of inspirational poetry.

Editor: Ellen Kleiner
Book design and production: Nicholas Morrow and Angela Werneke

Printed in China by South China Printing Co., Ltd.

Publisher's Cataloging-in-Publication Data

Morrow, Nicholas Michael.

    Songs to the beloved and her lovers / Nicholas Michael Morrow. --
1st ed. -- Taos, New Mexico : Gaia Grove Publishing, 2007.

        p. ; cm.
        (Songs of love ; one)
        ISBN-13: 978-0-9787977-0-6
        ISBN-10: 0-9787977-0-1
        Love poems rendered in the tradition of the mystic poets.
        Includes index.

        1. Love poetry. 2. Mysticism--Poetry.
        I. Title.

PS3613.O776 S66 2007   2006932410
811.6--dc22   0702

10 9 8 7 6 5 4 3 2 1

Dedication

Weaver or wizard
of the age of love—
read, speak, sing
these songs of praise
and place them
on the altar of your heart.

Soar on wings of devotion
as we journey together
through the realms of love,
where earth's glorious body
springs to life
as an abundant goddess
illumined by the sun.

Sound a call for lovers
to gather in the rainbow
light of a new day,
embracing singers and poets,
dancers and artists with vision.

Entrust these songs
to your majestic imagination
to create consciousness
for awakening.

IN GRATITUDE . . .

I offer my gratitude to the following authors, whose work has brought joy and inspiration to my writing. Much appreciation goes to Paramahansa Yogananda, whose *Rubaiyat of Omar Khayyam Explained* transformed my understanding of that great classic, and Llewellyn Vaughan-Lee, for his *Bond with the Beloved*. Special thanks go to Coleman Barks, Daniel Ladinsky, Kabir Helminski, Annemarie Schimmel, and others for awakening my Sufi heart. I extend appreciation as well to Stephen Mitchell, for his eloquent translations of Rainer Maria Rilke; Mary Oliver, for her stunning poetry; and Robert Bly, for revealing the romance and mysteries of life.

Recognition is given to Ellen Kleiner, my editor, and Angela Werneke, responsible for book design and production, for their artistic skills, patience, and perseverance. Without them this book would not have happened.

First and last, I give my appreciation to my family and to my wife, MariAnna Lands, for their love, support, and encouragement.

CONTENTS

—— The Seven Rays of Love ——

Rays of Love

Seven rays of love embrace earth,
illuminating the beloved's poetry.

Lovers weave geometries
with their wings of light
and ride fiery chariots
through the lush meadows
of their imagination.

Journey with us
through the realms of love,
opening your heart
with songs of devotion
for the beloved.

Speak these words of rapture
to those you adore,
with the passion of a lover
who sees everything
as the beloved,
revealing the primal truths
of your being.

The Seven Rays
of Love

BELOVED

Enter here,
the beloved's realm,
and soar on wings of devotion
along the blue ray of love
with your heart open
to her love.

The Beloved Approaches

In stillness,
in overwhelming emptiness,
there is excitement,
sensation whispering to our bodies,
rippling on the surface
of our souls.

The beloved approaches,
watching,
waiting for the opportunity
to enter our hearts
and summon a cosmos of love.

As her energy fills the air,
shining out of every living thing,
earth's crystalline substance
begins to glow.

We witness the beauty
in the warmth of her presence
and a symphony resounds
throughout existence.

When we shine like the sun,
these illusions,
the sweetness of life,
the ecstasy our bodies enjoy,
reflect her infinite oneness.

Dreamer and dream,
arise in each other
out of the stillness.

Lover and love
become the beloved,
emptiness,
full and alive.

Slight Chance

There is a chance
we will meet the beloved today,
so we look for a sign
as we descend to earth.

A birdcall at dawn,
awakens everyone
to the suspense.

We feel our hearts opening,
alerting our senses to her presence.

Remember when we were children
getting into mischief in heaven?

Remember when we were dolphins
singing and swimming in the ocean,
sounding our call to the stars?

Now we stalk the beloved
to reveal the mystery of love,
exploring intimacy on the inside,
with the slight chance
of becoming lovers
somewhere in paradise.

Welcome

Welcome to the temple of love.
Sacrifice self and appearances
so you may render with compassion
stories of the beloved and her lovers.

Enter the doorway of life
and become an emissary for beauty,
traveling in realms of light
with a new language and vision.

Embrace earth and heaven
in gratitude and praise,
with a song on your lips
and hope in your heart.

Sing the story of love
in the intimacy
of separation and reunion,
in the mystery of being lovers
in the garden of delight.

Enter the absolute present,
slipping between the veils
that separate us from the beloved.

Our bodies resonate with the stars,
receiving and sending light
in a universe of love.

Primal substance
matures in love's cauldron,
becoming conscious,
like a drop in the ocean
experiences the infinite,
like the ocean,
holding a drop in her arms,
becomes aware of herself.

Earth embodies the beloved
in a robe of green abundance,
everywhere a garden,
with us caring for the fragrance.

Write the story of creation
and live in the pages
as warriors of light.

Explore your passion
with your own particular spark
woven in the splendor of life.

Lovers bring their vitality
to the pageant of awakening,
giving consciousness sensuality
to partake in the ecstasy of love.

Mystic poets appear
in every chapter of existence,
singing and dancing
with their majestic imagination.

Listen to the gentle voices
of everything around you
and know the mood of the stars.

Live the fiery breath
of transformation
as you experience an evening breeze
or sunrise over a golden sea.

Land of Ma

Sing to us, O muse,
of the land of ma
and of lovers who dance
in the presence of the beloved.

Sing to us of the garden,
its wonders and delights,
of children who grow
in beauty and grace
and beings who play the earth
like a fine instrument
in a cosmic symphony.

Sing the saga of healing
and our opening to love,
serving the beloved.

Sing the joy of awakening,
weaving a web of compassion
throughout the land of ma.

Sing the lyrics
in a language of love,
inviting hearts to speak
in truth and clarity.

Mystic of Our Hearts

Who speaks through us
with love and adoration
for the world in which we live?

The story reverberates
in every action and deed—
a fragment of the one
whose grace fills the infinite.

The mystic of our hearts
sings love songs to existence,
and we do not exist.

We apprehend our oneness,
touching each other a thousand ways
to discover who we are
in the book of love.

The sun penetrates darkness,
becoming dawn and dusk,
spreading her blanket
under the stars.

We fade in the brilliance
as the beloved speaks
ecstatic poetry through us.

Perfect Mirror

Poetry accompanies us
on this mysterious journey,
opening doors to the unknown.

Innocent and transparent,
we merge freely with soul being,
going wherever she goes.

Knowing embraces the infinite,
like a drop that enters the sea
becomes the sea,
like breath merging with wind
touches the earth everywhere.

She mingles with the
beloved's original intention,
carried by our thoughts
into spirit realms.

She delights in every experience
on the path of life,
as our eternal partner,
transmitter and receiver,
the perfect mirror
and our most intimate lover.

We soar on wings of devotion,
creating poetry that resounds
through existence,
sleeping in each other's arms,
our souls radiant
and satisfied.

Naked Again

Poetry connects us
to the center of our love,
where the lucid image
of absolute beauty
permeates our essence
and we are naked again
in paradise.

The Beloved's Garden

Presences smile
as we enter their world,
a bustle of activity
with everything in balance.

Flowers greet the dawn
in mountain meadows,
where ceremonies of another kind
fill the night.

Trees return to their bodies,
energized by celestial spheres,
and star beings gather
to distribute codes of creation.

As we witness the magnificence,
the beloved opens her heavenly arms
to embrace her lovers.

The scent of love fills the air
with the passion of our embrace
as we wake
in the beloved's garden.

Grace and Abundance

Our friend comes a long way
to visit this abode
where we slowly wake
to the beloved as ourselves,
agreeing to tend realities
until dense ones become light.

She knows this way well,
traversing the path with intention,
dressed in beauty and grace,
seeking a lover
with kisses sweet as honey.

The brilliance of dawn,
clouds dancing in a blue sky,
and stars witnessing the mischief
activate our imagination.

From the chamber of love
comes poetry's seductive call,
and play from all directions
defines our being.

What else can we do
but open to the grace and abundance
our friend brings to share.

The Vast Chamber

We look through a doorway
from the bundles of our bodies,
created to know every facet
of the beloved,
becoming still
as we enter the vast chamber
of her heart.

We speak of eternal bliss
and the revelation of oneness,
of love and the divine script,
written a thousand different ways
to fulfill our mission.

Open the doors of paradise,
tear down walls and buttresses,
granting us freedom
to be lovers
enchanted by beauty,
naked and innocent.

Her smile,
the gentle rain that releases her scent,
a kiss from our sweet lips,
brings the dream to life.

We recognize each other
from primal beginnings,
when she conceived separateness
to experience union
through us.

Infinite Beauty

We find ways to touch
that arouse sensations
still resonating
from the moment of creation,
remembering
the infinite beauty
of the beloved's body.

Nebula of Love

Feel the whiteness of winter,
like being inside light
where shadow does not exist.

Colors appear,
pulsing,
weaving with one another,
evoking our imagination.

Our souls incarnate
without physical substance,
hunger, or thirst,
as wonder and curiosity
pound in our ethereal hearts,
resounding in song.

The beloved dresses in red
surrounded by gold,
with a blue and purple hue
held in emerald green.

Colors flow in ecstasy,
as rivers of compassion
merge like twin stars
dancing in a nebula of love.

Full of Lovers

The beloved comes for us!

She is a huntress
and we are her prey.

She sets traps
and baits them with sweet delicacies
to arouse our desire.

She creates decoys of immense beauty
and we follow each one
with blind abandon.

She whispers to us from the wilderness
with allure so potent
that we enter the wild unknown
without reason.

She captivates us
with her love,
calling us to her enchantment
until her realm teems with lovers.

Mystic Union

The voice of the mystic lover
wafts from the moon.
When we gaze at her face,
becoming quiet and still,
we know that fairies
dance in the garden.

Our bodies swell
in the buoyancy of love,
as if the air had hands.
The earth opens to intimacy
and trees sway,
singing with the breeze.

We bask in the magic,
light shimmering on our bodies
and eyes sparkling with mischief.
We enter passionate waters
and merge with the current,
embracing the beloved.

Drums beat
and fairies dance in the moonlight
as we perform
the rite of mystic union.

Whispering Softly

We speak a language of love
with honey on our lips
and our minds imagining the beloved
in sublime form.

What better task exists
than to resonate with each word,
creating poetry and song?

We speak our mother's tongue
and see with her eyes.
We speak the beloved's infinite wisdom
when truth lives in our hearts.

What task remains
when delusions fade away,
except to transcend reality
with vibrations of love.

We learn to articulate
like the fragrance of a rose,
whispering softly
in the language of love.

Fairy Tale of Life

The goddess pursues us every moment
and when our guard is down
she enters our hearts,
stirring up mischief.

Her song pulses in us,
and all our relations
sing the harmony.

We no longer see the prize
when we follow illusion
without realizing the extent
of her beauty.

She entered on the first day
and resides in our house,
having outrageous parties
without permission.

She awakens in the midst of our lives
and we become lovers,
like trees,
birds, and mountain meadows—
like her,
in this fairy tale of life.

Fully Dressed

You hide behind a cloud,
waiting for darkness
to expose your shining face.

We see you through an opening
without your dress,
rehearsing for a performance.

You bow and spin in every direction,
sending trails of light
into the darkness.

The beloved pulses in you
and earth witnesses the intimacy,
yielding to your eternal rhythm.

We know who you are,
ripped from our breasts
and placed in the night sky.

Fully dressed,
riding your golden chariot,
you reveal the secrets of love.

A Small Voice

Beloved,
someone asked
us to give you away
and we found ourselves holding on,
as if this small voice
mattered.

From your immortal being
you craft the cosmos,
reflecting magnificence,
and we believe in the illusion
that you are our possession.

You dwell in the infinite,
watching, allowing,
activating the voice in us
to join your divine chorus
residing in our hearts.

We enter the wilderness
and you lead us to loving arms,
honing our inspiration,
tuning our special frequency—
a small voice
somewhere in paradise.

Embellishing Her Imagination

The mother of all that is gives birth—
each unfolding into the next
with beauty and grace.

The soul imbues light with presence
and she envisions us in her glory,
a language of freedom,
passion, and love.

With each encounter
we invite exploration and intimacy,
weaving the beloved's tapestry.

We explore pathways of the heart,
embellishing her sublime imagination
with ecstasy and bliss.

Mated for Life

Speak to us;
don't leave us alone!

This cry resounds
from the beloved's nest
to the beloved
who dwells within and without,
filling space and time,
from us,
who taste her sweet nectar
and long for more.

Our cry rides the wind,
fructifying valley and mountain,
flowing to the beloved
on the strings
of her celestial harp.

We behold her splendor,
and the fabric of light about us
ignites in a thousand suns.

The fusion of our souls
sets waves upon the ocean,
ripples upon the web of destiny,
surrounding the earth with love.

High over the land we soar,
mated for life,
spiraling about each other
and answering the plea of her lovers
with cries of ecstasy.

Our Lips Meet

We cover the beloved
from head to toe in kisses.
Our lips meet
and our bodies burn
with devotion.

Soft Delicate Truths

Dearest beloved,
we have concern for this life,
where hard reality demands
so much attention
and we must hide to partake
of the soft delicate truths
of your being.

Hold us close to your breast
and stroke our fears,
alerting the universe
that change is at hand.

We rejoice in tranquility
with our minds still and active
in the same moment,
allowing the mystery room to play.

Our cup forgot long ago
the feeling of emptiness,
your blessings in continuous flow
with us busy passing them on,
dreaming still
of a world without pain.

The dream lives in us,
traveling between worlds
where love unites lover
and beloved.

We wake with the earth
in a cosmic initiation,
holding the frequency for love,
your soft delicate truths
blossoming in the garden.

Give It All

When the beloved arrives,
she expects a hug.

Give it!
Give it all!

Storyteller and Beloved

What is your story, beloved?

We honor and adore you,
following you everywhere
to hear your divine word.

Your story fills us
and we sing
the saga of awakening.

Whisper the juicy details of birth
and how we each grow
into a rose of sublime beauty.

Speak with the intimacy
of a lover,
as we hold you close,
breathing your fragrance.

Our stories blend and cease,
merging in the ecstasy,
storyteller and beloved
becoming the story.

Enter Our House

You enter our house
and we rise like leavened bread
in a warm oven.

We drink your sweet wine
and see visions of harmony
uniting realms.

The seasons come and go,
unfolding with the pulsing
of our hearts.

You envelop the infinite
and we breathe the pristine air
that unites worlds.

We discover love
and become your beloved,
opening like a flower
with the rising sun.

Nightingale of Our Hearts

My love for you is a child.
Your warm body next to mine
fills me with waves of bliss,
pure sensation, rendering me
unable to speak of love.

I love you
resounds in our hearts,
like birdsong at dusk,
inviting an ocean
to tickle our souls.

I love you,
I love you—
a call of lovers
clothed in a single sheath,
activating the magic of union.

Listen to earth's heartbeat
and sense her ecstasy
as we hold her
in our passionate arms,
singing to her beloved,
filling galaxies with light.

Time and space dissolve in oneness
and we live the majesty,
our sweet resonance
becoming an elixir of love,
creating touchstones
for the beloved.

Her touch is our embrace,
and when we kiss,
her sacred twin
becomes whole again.

I love you,
I love you
echoes throughout existence.

This mystery is the
nightingale of our hearts.

Spies for the Beloved

The illumined one enters the garden,
sensing presences
who have come for the fragrance.

Who are you
and why are you here?
asks the illumined one.

We are spies,
O radiant one;
we are spies for the beloved,
come to sing in the choir,
to listen to the resonance
of simplicity and truth,
to smell the aroma of souls
becoming sweet,
to witness the weaving of light
'midst your sun and stars.

Our senses transmute
compassion and love to signals,
returning to the beloved
the sustenance for which she longs.

Her sacrifice calls for the gift
she cannot give herself.

First separateness,
then free will,
reflecting the essence of love
to the cosmos.

Relaxed and fulfilled,
she sleeps
and dreams us in her garden
once again.

Revealing the Secret

Listen with the vastness of being.
Gaze into the light-filled air.

I am within your grasp,
always, always.

Feel the beloved's embrace
turning us sweet and passionate.

When you are in my arms
the mystery blossoms.

Majesty surrounds us
with divine presence
that carries an ancient dream
of a world united in love.

Come to me
through the veils of separation,
innocent and alive.

We activate our human matrix,
bridge worlds,
traverse space and time,
approaching the threshold of truth.

I love you without reason,
always, always.

The beloved permeates our being
and we tingle with excitement,
ready for the celebration.

I am love,
resounding within the mystery.

We come from bliss
to live in the world
and make known the unknown,
revealing the secret
that gives birth to love.

Her Presence

She reveals her presence
in the silence,

in the hush
when heart and mind
have no distinction,

in nature's grand arena
of life and death,

in the clamor of the market,
where fear and competition
become language,

in celebrations of love
that resound with recognition
of our awesome purpose,

in us,
waking in the wilderness
and fanning the fires of love
to honor her presence.

Lover's Chorus

Love abides in the heart
and poetry on the lips
of the beloved,
enticing lovers to open the gate
so her elixir may flow.

We tap her virgin spring,
recording lyrics with kisses
and songs of praise,
inviting everyone to join
the lover's chorus.

The final hour has come
and a wave of passion
engulfs the land,
erasing history and leaving love,
an abundant earth,
and lovers
singing poetry to creation
from the beloved's lips.

PRAYER

Enter here,
the realm of prayer,
and soar on wings of gratitude
along the purple ray of love
with your voice open
to her song.

Poet-Goddess

Beloved,
our lives express your beauty
with joy in our breast,
brimming with song.

We witness your pulsing,
transforming us
into a poem of love.

Let us be the poet-goddess
of your heart,
singing to the stars.

Let the earth
express her perfect self
to the world,
as we cultivate the garden
for you and your lovers.

Pulsations of Love

We love you,
beloved.

We bathe in your glory
and draw it gently about us,
like a shawl of light.

Our hearts take over our bodies
and we see you everywhere.

Even the mountains reach
for the sky
like voluptuous breasts
to nourish the cosmos.

Your presence devours separateness,
filling us with devotion
and pulsations of love.

Brilliant Sun

Rise up and greet the dawn!
She comes for us,
disturbing us in our sleep,
and will not cease till we wake.

Look how she illuminates the world
so we may experience
sublime truth.

Feel her enter us,
moving about with inner touch,
filling us with compassion.

She spreads a web of wonder
on the path we tread
and our gifts flow to earth
as seeds for her garden.

We receive love and its antidote
in each other,
a wheel in perpetual motion.

We are twin stars,
spinning night into day,
living in her infinite universe.

She comes for us
and we show her the way,
opening the door to our hearts
and placing there
a brilliant sun.

Overflowing

The beloved answers our prayer
with joy that is overflowing
and wherever we go
she embraces us
with ecstasy.

Mixing Light and Love

Come to the heart of your inner eye,
mixing light and love
with sublime inspiration.

Enter the tavern without walls,
where a congregation of souls
gathers every night
to sing the beloved's poetry.

Build a radiant web of light
to surround the earth
like a mother
holding her newborn child.

Pray for the moment
when veils of fear, hate, and greed
become transparent.

What if we desire the same thing?

What if we see with eyes of love
the beloved's glory in each other?

What if love rules the earth
and we are free to express
our special talents?

Flowers will blossom in the garden
and seasons will pulse with passion,
giving birth to beauty.

Abundance will emerge from our care,
as food and shelter spring
from our intentionality.

Pilgrims will arrive from the stars,
moving through dimensions
to experience earth's
special flavor of love.

Lovers will realize their gifts
and, performing miraculous deeds,
will apprehend her joy.

Come to the heart of your inner eye,
mixing light and love
in sublime inspiration.

Nodal Points of Light

The beloved expresses herself
through our miraculous bodies,
honoring us with the invitation
to contribute to her creation.

Our centers align with her
cosmic strands
and beams of light
radiate in all directions
from our crystal essence.

We place ourselves at nodal points
throughout the mystic web,
encompassing the earth
as emissaries of love,
modeling a matrix for union.

We resonate with the stars,
as lovers join hands and hearts,
generating a living,
pulsing sacred geometry.

We become the prayer,
the source of her immortality,
singing these songs of love.

Our bodies merge,
becoming whole and alive
to participate in the sweetness
of union.

We find ways of being
that awaken passion,
sending ripples through
our receptive fabric,
emanating ecstasy to the cosmos
from our nodal points of light.

Enter in Gratitude

Enter in gratitude,
for the beloved lives here
and her light and love
sustain the world.

We tend the garden
with her humble servants,
who adore and care for her
with each breath and heartbeat.

Her beauty radiates from everything
that is wild and free.

We know the story of passion
in our hearts,
and burn with desire
when the beloved is near.

We enter her holy shrine
where lovers greet us,
smiling with anticipation,
absorbed in prayer.

Listen to Birds

Give over to the beloved.
Her presence heals every hesitation,
like breath
blending with sky.

She activates us with love,
turning us into lovers
singing with every breath
songs of adoration.

She inspires us with beauty
and stimulates our imagination.

Resonance lives in us,
awakened by a gesture of love
that bursts into song.

Listen to birds.

They find ways
to praise the beloved
with every note.

Their poetry rides the wind
as they fly.

The Language of Love

In the language of love
each verse stands alone
speaking to our souls.

Having just been born,
we know nothing
and every experience is our first.

Forgive us for our clumsiness
and this crude communication,
knowing our love is true.

The beloved is sweet,
like cherry juice
running down our chins
on a warm spring day.

Our vibrations merge with
celestial spheres,
orchestrating star symphonies
for the beloved.

Innocence is transparent
in the sun's light,
illumined through inspiration,
lived with the purity of desire.

Priest and priestess meet,
celebrating intimacy,
solving the mystery.

As we behold beauty about us,
duality dissolves
and we become infinite.

Who can speak of the beloved
and apprehend her spirit,
if not our eternal self?

This way of being together
begins a pilgrimage
leading to enlightenment.

When all we want to do
is make love,
the universe cries
yes
to her beloved.

Take us in like warm liquid
and feel our pulse
defining the unknown.

These bodies
fit together with perfection
and organize the stars
into constellations.

Poetry expresses the primeval urge
to transform words of fear
into butterflies of light.

We partake of sacred communion,
weaving the beloved's garment
from threads of remembrance.

To experience the infinite present
we activate compassion
that, when realized,
turns to bliss.

We are not the same substance,
separated out as man and woman,
but two becoming one,
creation itself.

The beloved perfects mortality
with her whole body;
we are that perfection.

Our father is a geometrician,
a lens through which
the cosmos enters
our mother's womb.

We defy the idea of duality,
giving form to light
that dances between worlds.

Timelessness shatters apparent reality
and veils lift in all directions,
expanding our horizons.

Father Sky and Mother Earth,
in continuous play and creativity,
imbue these bodies
with living substance
and sacred geometry.

Without resistance,
who knows who is who?
Your touch, my skin,
our pulsing bodies of passion
igniting the night sky.

We sit before the altar
holding the beloved's jewels,
with her gift of compassion
forming a matrix for ascension.

Musicians gather in the garden,
tuning their instruments
to the first rays of dawn,
preparing for the wedding.

Prayer captures the essence of love
like a playful enchantress
quickens the beloved's heart.

Preparing for Flight

In gratitude, we stand
at the dawning of a new age,
ready to meet the unknown.

Consciousness gives form to reality,
exploring unlimited possibilities
in a sympathetic universe.

Love dresses in many colors
dancing on the surface of our souls,
shimmering with delight.

The beloved approaches,
beckoning us to express our love
through the intimacy we share.

Her presence brings joy
and we spread our wings,
preparing for flight.

Compassion and Infinite Bliss

Quan Yin,
mother of compassion and infinite bliss,
beholds the fields where children play,
offering love as a participant
in the story of human evolution.

We enter the garden,
caretakers of her beauty,
weaving a powerful matrix
as a web of protection
for the earth.

We build the temple
with wonder and delight,
singing and dancing
her eternal praise.

Dearest beloved,
ancient mother and lover,
you are the ocean and mountain,
the holy room where we worship,
the window and grove beyond.

We come to you
naked and vulnerable,
caressing your perfect breasts,
arousing passion
so milk may flow.

We have tasted your love,
like a star
held in arms of light,
like a mother
ripped open with joy and pain
or a father holding the fruit
of creation.

Stillness covers the earth
and we sing songs of love,
soothing your heart
of compassion and infinite bliss.

Celebrating Existence

There is magic in her love,
bestowing on the earth
her holy essence.

We reside in her sanctuary,
where sacred beings dwell,
to discover who we are.

We live in the world
without destroying the beauty
and power of creation.

We learn the language of love
and become magicians,
wearing her jeweled cloak.

The blessing of her embrace
brings us to this enchantment
where we are lovers
in her garden.

We proclaim her immortality
as we thrive in these bodies,
communities of beings
celebrating existence.

Apprehending the Infinite

We pray for love
to quicken our hearts
and refresh our souls.

We rise in rarefied air
of the beloved's presence,
apprehending the infinite.

Her light surrounds us
when we surrender to her will,
meeting the impossible
with courage and grace.

We sow seeds in the wilderness,
giving birth to innocence,
bringing hope to her children.

Peace encompasses earth,
as sublime expressions of love
flow in every heart.

With thanksgiving and praise,
we perceive everything
as the beloved.

Serving the Beloved

The child wants to know what we do.

On the hilltop a college stands.
What do they do there?

Below lies a town and lake
holding clues to the mystery.

Lovers always look for love
to celebrate existence,
living in joy
and adoration of the beloved.

What has the earth come to do?

Look at her,
willing to be a garden
where we raise our children
and create abundance.

She is a child in another garden,
growing in her mother's arms,
learning to express
her special quality of soul.

Is it possible that we are here
to make the earth beautiful
so she may sing her song?

This is what we do
serving the beloved.

Love Lays Bare

Describe the longing
that knows the beloved
and use the language of love,
for longing knows who we are
and love lays bare the heart,
where hopes and dreams
are conceived.

Gratitude and Praise

We come in silence,
freeing her voice of compassion
to speak to our hearts.

We are her children
for generations in all directions.

Hear our prayer
for love to enter every being
and heal earth's pain.

Forgiving ourselves for being separate,
we become whole again.

Gratitude and praise fill us
forever,
ever and ever.

United with the Beloved

This breath and passion for life
stimulate our senses,
cultivate innocence,
and activate truth.

We pray for stillness
to dispel illusion
as the beloved
holds us in her awareness.

Love allows everything
and guides us through the fire,
burning resistance to ash,
as we open the door to freedom,
uniting with the beloved.

TEACHING

Enter here,
the realm of teaching,
and soar on wings of trust
along the magenta ray of love
with your mind open
to her thoughts.

The Harvest

We emerge from the illusion
of being priest and priestess
to the realization that we
are simply lovers
tempering the fires of love.

We arrive at the edge of existence
seeking balance in our lives,
forging possibility from illusion
and reality with choices
we have made.

The beloved cultivates the garden
with wisdom and grace
and her life pulses in us,
bringing movement and sound,
joy and sorrow
to the earth.

She reaps the harvest
as we grow ripe and sweet,
returning unconditionally
to her.

Ecstasy within Time

The beloved enters our hearts
like an ocean,
revealing the secret of everlasting life.

This wondrous organ in the breast
pulses in unison with creation,
like the earth
beneath wind and tides.

Beyond the present,
beginnings and endings do not exist.

We spend every moment making love,
and worlds within worlds
come into being.

The intimacy of our embrace
quickens the moment,
ecstasy within time,
eternity itself.

Light Begets Light

A torch of love frees the lover
to know the beloved,
and the source originates
beyond physical forms.

We cast a circle of power,
channeling a column of light
directly from spirit.

We know in our minds
what incarnation teaches us;
now, another knowing
enters our hearts.

The cells in our bodies
are blessed with memory
and our crystal strands
resonate with eternity.

The path is through the heart,
allowing love to transform thoughts
into native cosmic intelligence.

We enter the heart with compassion,
forgiving, letting go,
and becoming transparent.

We serve the beloved
by supporting her lovers to love.

We burn with love
naked before the beloved,
so she may access the source
in us.

In meadow or grove
where sacred rings endure,
we lie on the earth,
absorbing the potency
and consciousness
of the eternal.

We rise up in silence,
connected and alive,
carrying a torch of love
for the earth and her lovers.

Her light shines in us,
as light begets light.

Prepare Your Fabric

Remember,
consciousness creates reality.

Focus on the task;
be still and listen,
enjoying the love that flows
and enlightens the mind.

The being of earth feels
an emotion you call fear
with only a hint of freedom,
realizing that transformation
is at hand.

Earth entreats you to prepare
for awakening,
by cleansing your mind and body
so light and love may flow.

She knows the meaning of birth
and the nature of truth,
entreating you to touch
separateness and oneness
simultaneously.

Prepare your fabric
to hold a frequency of love,
activating your crystal strands,
burning away fear in a moment.

There is a new orientation
in the cosmos,
where presences are seen,
taken in like breath,
preparing organs of love
for another birth.

The Gift

The gift flows
like water in the earth
in anticipation of reunion,
seeking to express herself.

The gift knows our soul,
wakened early with the sun
and excited by possibilities,
like eating strawberries
or swimming in the sea.

The gift senses our desire
for intimacy,
enlivening our bodies with passion,
singing songs of praise
to the beloved.

The gift offers opportunity,
blessing us with the potential
to participate in creation,
returning to her,
conscious and aware.

The gift wears a gown of glory
in her many ecstatic forms,
finding us wherever we are
and whispering secrets
to our hearts.

Sharing Intimacy

Very near the center,
we apprehend the world,
expanding to the infinite,
and find each other
in the vast unknown,
sharing intimacy and love.

Emissaries for Ecstasy

Speak to us
at the dawning of innocence,
when life is fresh
and we know only love.

Encourage us
and feel fingers delicately dance
over your surfaces,
where senses reach up,
like trees and mountains.

Look into our eyes
and transport us to paradise
with visions of peace and harmony
manifesting in the world.

Sing to us
with your wind and rain,
like a mother rocking her child
hums lullabies
composed by angels.

We are the privileged ones,
chosen to come to earth
as a miracle of spirit,
waking up to our
compassionate self.

Your intention echoes
in our souls
and we traverse the spheres
leaving stardust in our wake.

We are emissaries for ecstasy,
alive and free,
initiating the innocent
with signals from your heart.

Love

Love arrives with dawn,
soft and alive,
bringing color and light
to our lives.

She warms us with desire
as her creatures wake
and begin to dance.

Love enters and we glow
with the same radiance
that sparks creation.

Our souls merge
love into love,
layering existence
in new forms of beauty.

Wherever we go
the sun rises with dawn
and love releases her sweet scent
from the flowers
in our garden.

Shackles

The beloved comes
wheeling her hammer of compassion
to break the shackles
binding our hearts.

We are face-to-face
with the riddle,
in a final confrontation
with control.

We long for freedom
to express love with other beings,
nature, and presences,
where the language of love
caresses our imagination with songs
giving birth to passion.

We join in communion,
willing to shed our shackles,
and she comes
with her golden hammer,
freeing the fragrance
from our hearts.

Enveloping Time

Intimacy comes with our embrace,
enveloping time
like priest and priestess
entering mystic union.

Our love outgrows understanding
and leads us to the secret,
where language is a child
touching everything with awe
and wonder.

We dress in sun and moon,
shimmering on the ocean,
dancing with delight.

We create music,
playing like celestial spheres
resounding with the stars
in beams of rainbow light.

I love you
are the first words we speak,
as we enter the madness
and see each other
for the first time.

Smelling the Fragrance

We abide by the ocean
as the tide comes and goes
bringing gifts to shore.

We know her moods,
one moment ecstatic,
the next quiet and subdued.

We spend lifetimes here,
no more than a heartbeat
for the cosmos.

We unite in love,
like the land and the sea,
like space holding sun,
moon, and stars.

Majesty surrounds us,
reminding us of mortality,
proclaiming the eternal.

We live on a beach in paradise,
smelling the fragrance,
tides pulsing,
ecstasy rushing to shore.

Chariots of Ecstasy

Listen to the symphony
and know I am love,
the all-embracing oneness
that holds existence
like a newborn child.

We hear her music
on the shimmering fibers
that entwine our hearts,
chanting songs of love,
activating codes of creation.

She calls us to her enchantment,
transforming our lives
with the alchemy of love,
riding chariots of ecstasy
into an ingenious world.

Awakening the Lover

Lovers draw reality about them
on their journey to enlightenment.

Their language describes
what the heart sees
as they travel on life's path,
weaving beauty from passion.

We are lovers
on a crusade for freedom,
cutting through illusion
with the continuity of love.

We recite ecstatic poetry,
awakening the lover in every heart
to the presence of the beloved
in every thing.

Singing to Us

Beloved,
we hear your call
and cannot come.

Our hearts break
knowing we are not born.

A stick in the river
spins and, twirling with the current,
is drawn to shore,
while the river continues.

Don't be a stick;
be the river.
She becomes the ocean.

Listen to the tree
calling our name since we arrived.

She has a message from the earth,
whose heart holds the ocean
and the sky.

She has been waiting
to tell us who we are,
while we conjure distractions
to fill our infinite mind.

Be still and listen to her song
and know it's our souls
singing to us.

Forgiveness

Forgiveness dissolves truth
into compassion,
past sorrows into laughter,
and calls for a sacred council
with the beloved.

Prison Walls

We stand as prisoners
in the beloved's garden,
holding our torches high
to see over mighty walls
and beyond.

We play like horses
in a mountain meadow,
captivated by beauty,
returning to love
in every cycle of life.

Presences gather in the garden,
inspiring us with divine purpose,
motivating us to gather
stones for the beloved
and build a temple of light.

Silence gives its shelter,
holding and nurturing us
like a mother's womb,
until our voices become clear,
prompting us to sing.

We manifest from the same substance,
living in beauty and grace
in a garden that encircles us,
and these prison walls
are covered with flowers.

Bringing Us Close

There is no telling who we are
or where we come from,
for the doorways are infinite
and in constant change,
bringing us close
in the early-morning light
of a new day.

Voyages of the Heart

Many voyages of the heart
lead us on this magnificent journey.

Within breathes the mystery
and unfathomable beauty
of unconditional love.

We fashion beautiful things,
giving people joy and inspiration.

We birth children
and hold their children,
to experience sublime continuity.

No matter how much we are
loved from the outside,
longing resides in our hearts
to be touched from within.

Intimacy envelops us
as we travel through the universe
with the alchemy of love,
turned inside out.

Glimpse of Gold

Our souls,
excited by possibilities,
anticipate being together
with the ecstasy of our bodies
in the midst of life.

Consciousness dissipates at death
unless we cultivate transcendence,
moving between worlds at will
to meet on the other side.

We know what they look for,
lovers who tend the beloved
with selfless adoration.

What else but a glimpse of gold,
a sparkle in the eye,
or the hint of a smile
clothed in the elegance
of unconditional love.

Stop Playing Around

Stop playing around at being a lover
and go directly to the heart
of love.

Return to the beloved her gifts,
her sacred charms
and myths of greatness
beyond this impeccable moment.

Allow poetry to become child's talk,
mixing sound and wonder
into rhyme
that nature understands.

Give birth to language
that can warm her body
with intimacy and integrity.

Our words are love's hands,
caressing her with enthuiasm,
awakening truth and love
with poetry.

Let Go of Control

Let go of control
and allow yourself to be vulnerable,
at the mercy of the beloved.

Eddies form in the river,
exquisite vortexes
no one ever sees,
yet this activity brings life
to the garden.

Everything supports her plan.
Our hands and feet
fashion beauty wherever we go.
Our feelings establish a direct link
to her heart.
Our thoughts weave a tapestry
of divine love.

Let go of control
and allow destiny to unfold,
as her blessing imbues us
with dignity and grace.

Sounds of Sentience

Our voices open a door
to the beloved,
brimming with enthusiasm,
joy, and compassion.

The poet
builds path and temple,
serving a thousand guests
to speak a line of truth.

In a breath
eternity and the present
investigate infinite possibilities.

We play inside reality
as flowers open
and birdsong enlivens the air.

Sounds of sentience
evolve into a chorus of praise
as the beloved embraces creation.

Silence brings peace
and we merge without bodies
in infinite bliss.

Web of Wonder

Follow your heart
and weave a web of wonder
through paradise.

Merge with your soul,
becoming transparent
like a new moon.

Come with me
to the chamber of forgetfulness
and play as a child
excited to be born again.

Make love,
praising the beloved
with your sweet lips on mine.

Ceremony of Life

We enter layers of being
where the goddess is abundant,
blessing us with her love.

Senses are rarefied,
blending with one another,
as we merge in ecstasy.

Fear dissolves in her presence
and courage rules the day,
unveiling our souls' purpose.

Oceans and rivers pulse
through our mortal fabric
as our breath and the wind
caress the earth.

Every time we touch,
gazing into each other's eyes
to explore inner beauty,
a new language is born.

Listen to the rain
as it falls on fertile ground,
imbuing the earth with life.

Listen to our souls laughing
as they dance through the meadows
of wonder and delight.

Listen to poetry
as it wraps itself around
every star in the universe.

Listen to lovers
singing songs of adoration,
and to our love
remembering the temple
and ceremony of life.

Scent of a Rose

She enters your hands,
giving form to beauty.

She enters your voice,
singing melodies of love.

She enters your heart,
making you a mother.

You meet your soul in her,
a perfect reflection
of the goddess.

Flowers unveil your secrets
and you bathe in their fragrance.

Water them with joy
and feel the arms of the universe
gently holding you.

Know who you are
in every layer of your being,
bridging realities
with the scent of a rose.

Secrets

We uncover secrets
hidden in our memory,
revealing who we are.

The beloved's thoughts,
sensations, and feelings
are ours.

Separateness can't exist
when all that is
comes from a single source.

Now we know
the greatest blessing—
twin souls spinning
about her sacred center.

A Clear View

There is always a clear view
to the beloved.

Be still and open
to beauty everywhere
and one shall catch
the eye of your heart.

Take it into your being,
calling your lover to life
and sacrifice resistance
in the fires of love.

We are vantage points
with a view to the beloved,
our eyes on each other
and our bodies
trembling with excitement.

River Knows

The river knows our feelings
better than we do.

Listen to her—
she knows who we are.

When we speak her language,
we know, as well.

Infinite Compassion

To love myself,
I must love you.

To love you,
I must love myself.

Infinite compassion
in a human heart.

PASSION

Enter here,
the realm of passion,
and soar on wings of creation
along the red ray of love
with your spine open
to her fire.

Bag Full of Kisses

We come to steal a kiss
and you pretend not to notice.

We begin to explore possibilities
and you leave jewels
on our path.

We share your essence
and images melt into life,
fully clothed in wonder,
pulsing with anticipation.

You knew we would come this way
and saw our bag full of kisses
with your name on it.

What else could have brought us here,
other than the business of love
and your lips,
ready for celebration?

Your flower opens
and we delight in the fragrance,
poised,
with our bag full of kisses.

Beauty of Love

My love,
how would you like to be served today?

Like a child
watching fairies
on leaves in the garden
after a gentle rain
and not being told their names?

Like a fire
giving warmth and passion,
until screams
fill the world with ecstasy?

Like a lover
whose lips fold with mine,
awakening every creature
in our being,
gently stroking the soft fur
of our souls?

Come to my chamber
and cavort for eternity,
getting lost
in the beauty of love.

Eyes of Passion

Night is a mysterious lover,
using eyes other than light
to perceive the beloved.

The foreplay of dusk
sets the tone for romance
and crickets string their violins
for an evening of love.

We are the first to arrive,
building the temple
and purifying the hearth.

Stars come with darkness
and a moon
to accentuate the beauty.

Exploration begins
with a stroke and a sigh,
followed by expressions of love
that no words can describe.

Come into the night,
my beloved,
and unveil the mystery
with eyes of passion.

Tickling Sentience

You dress like a flower,
and fragrance
announces your presence.

You grow in mountain meadows
and summon the wind,
sending us over the earth,
tumbling with enthusiasm.

You call for the rain,
giving fairies baths,
awakening spirits everywhere
with life's sweet smells.

Rapture abounds in us,
tickling sentience
with a kiss.

Perfect Love

From the beginning of time
lovers have gathered
to celebrate their passion.

We spring from that ancient race,
remembering how to pray
and conceive sublime beauty.

When our eyes meet,
exciting our memory,
and we caress each other
with tender devotion,
a river of ecstatic poetry
flows through us.

It takes a lifetime
to become a poet
and fulfill our mission.

It takes a moment
to live the poem
of perfect love.

Bodies of Light

You reside in us.
We go there to be with you,
to satisfy our longing
and become your dream.

We are empty and full
in the same moment,
like a breath,
expanding to fill the cosmos
and contracting to primal
existence.

We hold you close,
kneading your body like soft clay,
covering your face with kisses,
as passion surges
through our bodies of light.

The universe is ecstatic
to have twin stars in the family,
dissolving separateness,
dancing in the night sky.

Laughing Light

You comfort us with compassion
and surround us with a cloak
of love and inspiration.

We hear a nightingale
singing your song
and a chorus of lovers
speaking your word.

Light the altar and open a way
for souls to travel upon,
entering new dimensions
with balance and grace.

Feel the excitement of being free
and supported to share passion
with each other.

Come to my heart's chamber
and experience the majesty
of my sublime imagination.

Ride your chariots of fire
and meet me in the dawning
of a new day,
illuminating night's mystery.

Feel your bodies respond to touch
and the bliss beyond touch,
spinning in pools of laughing light.

We claim our true occupation,
living the wonder of creation,
birthing worlds
of adoration and praise.

Tuning Fork for Love

We are a tuning fork for love,
vibrating with the beloved's hand
as she embraces life.

She honors our desire,
willing to be a guide
on the path of enlightenment,
as we surrender to her.

Our presence enlivens the garden
and her musicians play
a new world into form.

We express our essence
in every chapter of existence,
vibrating still,
a tuning fork for love.

Edge of Existence

The warmth of your body
entwined with mine
on cold winter mornings
envelops me in bliss.

Close
like an ocean,
our tides mingle,
activating the rise and fall
of creation.

A deep glow emanates
from the coals of our sacred fire,
defining the edge of existence.

Love Lights up the Night

What words infuse a poem with love
like the call of a mourning dove,
like a heartfelt blessing fills
the garden with her daffodils?

Who sounds the wake-up call
dissolving every fear and lie,
lifting truth into the light
to give us clarity and sight?

We come to her breast,
seeking long-awaited rest
from the joy of sentience,
in the midst of magnificence.

We enter her holy womb,
rising like the harvest moon,
exploding like a brilliant sun,
as the goal of peace is won.

We carry her sacred seed
sown in earth alive and free,
speaking poetry with delight
as love lights up the night.

Disturbing Containment

Containment is difficult
in situations like this.

We fill an opening
and another appears,
then another,
keeping up with our willingness
for communion.

A single sunrise circles the earth,
greeting old friends with a new face
every day.

A single feeling unites us,
disturbing containment
with cries of ecstasy.

Pure Rose Wine

The craft is in the river
where currents grow strong,
as cascading water sings
the beloved's birthing song.

Wonder at her hopes and dreams
as she gives us wings to fly.
Listen to the sounds of spring
calling from the sky.

Come to us a rainbow
of dancing, shimmering light
and we will take you on our craft
of wonder and delight.

Come to us still a bud
growing sweet in her womb
and we will be your lover
calling to the moon.

Come to us a goddess
dressed as abundant earth
and we will plow your holy fields,
preparing for another birth.

Feel the liquid pearls of passion
rising up our spines
and the sweetness of our lips
from her pure rose wine.

The craft is in the river
whose currents now come to rest,
as you and I grow silent,
her child in our breast.

Bathe in the Splendor

If we give everything for love,
what is left?

There remains an emptiness so vast
that existence seems a mere drop
in the sea.

This drop,
sweet as honey,
merges with the infinite,
eliciting a smile on her face,
laughter in the cosmos
and compassion in our hearts.

Why question death and birth?

Rather, allow love to flow
from your breast to the beloved,
who resides in every atom
of the universe.

Our eyes burn for love,
like the sun's brilliance
seeks darkness for her lover.

When we kiss without expectation,
we bathe in the splendor
of the beloved's ecstasy.

When love empties from our hearts
the chalice begs to be filled,
again and again.

Give everything for love,
since all there is
is love.

Fires of Love

Every morning
upon waking to beauty,
we tend the fires of love.

When ashes accumulate
from transformation,
we spread them on barren soil
to feed the earth.

Flames dance on the surface
of our bodies,
leaping in the air
with joyous anticipation.

You spread before me,
curves of flesh and passion,
with a beautiful smile
and eyes of emerald green.

I am warm waters
at the shores of paradise,
filling every crevice of your being
and caressing your tender places.

Morning is our favorite time!

Our Special Fragrance

How can we put in words
the condition of being conscious,
of waking inside you,
realizing we also manifest love?

We write poetry to you,
for you are our lover,
the warmth and ecstasy
that pulses in our bodies,
the fragrance of a meadow
at dawn.

The mystery of love
has stolen our identity
and a river of passion
heads for the sea
with us in her wake.

You brought us here
and now we are wild and free,
exploring the vastness of life
with our special fragrance.

Language of Sensuality

The ocean sings with the wind,
messenger and lover,
giving their secrets away.

We pulse with their primal rhythms,
sending signals to the moon.

That is one way to say,
I love you.
We know another!

You must be completely still
and unsuspecting.

We come close,
caressing the sublime contours
of your body,
and bring our lips to yours,
forgetting everything.

Your breathing increases,
whistling against bare walls,
resounding in the chamber of love.

We speak like creation herself,
a language of sensuality,
finding ways to say,

I love you,
I love you.

⁓

All Night

We jugglers
keep time in suspension
to make the most of love,
finding that our kisses
last all night
like the stars.

The Sacred Grove

We dance in the grove
spinning with delight,
arms open to the sky,
primed for flight.

We trade our identity
for that of a mountain
covered with tall pines
singing in the breeze.

Your breath touches my cheeks
and we kindle the fire,
filling the earth with warmth.

I love you
echoes from stone cliffs
and sings with the rain,
giving birth to eternity.

When we touch
magic permeates the air,
making love-mischief
wherever we go.

You are the sacred twin
I came to find
and our meeting unites worlds.

Here, in the sacred grove
we build the temple
and light candles
for the celebration.

Crying Out

We come to you
with our whole beings
ripped open and exposed,
crying out,
like the ocean
kissing the shore.

Honoring the Beloved

We know love
as flame rips open our senses,
our elegant bodies
transformed in waves of light,
warming our souls.

We sleep
for thousands of years,
incubating the power of love,
the beloved's tool of creation.

In deep meditation
the hush of dawn
plans a magnificent sunrise,
as we wake in each other's arms
remembering our intimacy.

Desire rises in us,
forgiving every hesitation,
remembering ancient memories
in a timeless universe.

Our lips tremble,
eyes sparkling with anticipation,
as the excitement of love
devours our minds
with pulsing, passionate
screams of devotion,
honoring the beloved.

Completely Loved

You are in my arms,
kissing my face,
calling me beautiful,
twin soul
seeking the beloved's heart,
the sweetness of the goddess
when she is completely loved.

How Beauty Feels

Listen to the voice in the hearth.
Burn, burn, fire of the heart!
Make light out of substance
that comes from light.

The love we receive spends itself,
turning sublime beauty
into sublime beauty,
leaving joy and fulfillment.

Fine essence blends with love,
increasing as it is given.

Pouring ourselves into the beloved,
we become an open channel
for the ocean.

Listen to her
as her song fills the universe.

The mystery comes with desire
to be close and intimate,
to pulse with ecstasy
like the stars.

Savor the mystery
and come to the garden,
setting this moment
in the beloved's infinite eye.

Listen to the voice in the hearth
and know how beauty feels,
savoring these moments
for eternity.

Illusion

Only in being separate
can we love each other.

That also is illusion.

One Ecstatic Member

She comes when love is abundant
to experience intimacy.

She is the goddess
whose inner spaces we explore
when we make love.

Waves of passion surge in us
as we enter into communion
with her.

She sends us to explore
the edges of our love,
where the wine of life
blends with the mysteries
and secrets of union.

We use our imagination
and the tools of initiation
to transform consciousness
into bodies of light.

We trade places and identity is lost
as we enter the chamber of devotion,
becoming infinite and whole.

Twin galaxies reveal themselves,
appearing in the night sky
as one ecstatic member
in an expanding universe.

Look how they spin
in each other's arms,
sending light into the darkness
and cries of rapture
into the silence.

Songs of Devotion

Poetry reveals the unknown
with every breath
and ray of light.

She expresses with words of love,
reaching with heart's pure hands
to unveil the sacred
everywhere.

Come with truth and beauty,
sending prayers to the beloved
with every heartbeat.

Come with desire
surging through your body,
entering rivers of ecstatic poetry
where realms merge.

Songs of devotion
connect every particle
in the universe through us.

We live in the garden
and cultivate the fertile soil
from which poetry grows.

Beacons for Love

Exposed and transparent
we journey through the land,
leaving jewels in our wake.

Our thoughts weave realities
from our dreams
into stories for the beloved.

We converse like old lovers,
remembering the landscape
and sensitive places.

We embrace each other
with our fleshy sheaths
permeated with passion,
pores open and crying,
traveling in mystic union
with our souls
as beacons for love

Celebration of Spring

Kiss me like a rose kisses a bee.

I enter your fragrant petals
and bathe in your pollen,
ecstatic and unaware
of time or place.

Your nectar covers my body
with the oils of love
and you lay open,
exposed to my hunger
devouring every particle
of your being.

Your cries fill the garden
and a thousand petals engulf me
in an ocean of bliss.

No words remain to speak our love,
only the fragrance,
leaving poetry for lovers
in celebration of spring.

Our Awareness

My love,
I come to you in silence,
on the finest strand
of the beloved's hair.

I whisper your name
and you smile in your sleep,
as our souls dance and play.

I slip into your arms,
warm and alive,
activating waves of bliss.

I know you like I know myself
and we share the ultimate intimacy.

We enter heaven in a dream,
ghosts to illusion's eyes,
tasting the splendor
of our awareness.

Songs of Love

In the beginning, love ruled,
yet to manifest
in her sublime form.

Pure power surged in her
with potential to become infinite
from the inside out.

She played and danced,
permeating life with her
subtle fluids,
creating music and harmony.

Conscious of herself
she was everywhere at once,
weaving beauty
into a web of awareness.

We are messengers
bringing her matrix to earth,
manifesting with heaven
these songs of love.

Our Love

Our love rises
in the dark of winter,
in the brilliance
emanating from your presence.

We follow our love,
for we know
she has the gift we came to find.

Our love is a fine dress,
becoming transparent,
and everywhere we go
we are naked and exposed.

Our love gets excited
when you are near,
and will not behave,
taking us on wild excursions.

We live in the presence of beauty,
sharing our love with everything,
the sunrise and ocean
surging through us.

To Touch the Sky

Come naked and alive,
pressing your body to mine
as our souls dance and sing,
moving with rhythm and rhyme.

How else can it be
when lovers meet
playing in the apple tree?

How else can it be,
earth and sea
pulsing with her mystery?

We drink her sacred wine
and harvest fruit from her tree
creating an elixir for love,
setting the galaxy free.

How grand this space we travel,
exploring the blessings of love;
what wonder our kisses and cries
as we expand to touch the sky.

Ripe Fruit

Don't be afraid to let go
of the barrier that separates us
from the infinite.

Surrender tears us apart
dispersing our identity with the wind,
becoming a breath
on the face of time.

We merge in landscapes
beyond our imagination,
where substance condenses
from our creative passion.

Beauty expresses herself
in the air we breathe,
in a moonbeam on the sea,
in the sweetness of ripe fruit,
with you and I
inside each other.

Seasons of Love

She wears many faces
that peel away with the seasons.

The one we give our life for
lies beyond illusion,
transparent,
sometimes the reflection
holding us close,
sometimes kissing our tears.

Love wears the final mask,
beyond which
consciousness is not experienced.

We go there and return
with smiles on our faces,
knowing the truth of being.

She creates us
as innocent parts of herself,
free to explore the intricacies
of union.

We discover that our parts
match perfectly.

Joyfully we fit together
in the warmth of her embrace
through all the seasons of love.

Ecstatic Dolphins

Come to me, my love,
in any disguise you dream up
and I will remove the veils
until there is only you,
naked, vulnerable,
desiring me,
like an ocean of ecstatic dolphins.

JOURNEY

Enter here,
the realm of your journey,
and soar on the wings of courage
along the rose-gold ray of love
with your vision open
to her light.

Path of Love

We come to the path of love
without a map for our minds,
where doors to the halls of glory
are crafted from the story of man.

We know that everything
these senses perceive
is the substance of reality,
and where our souls go
is beyond this,
revealed in ancient language.

The path of love has a jewel
at the end of a rainbow,
yet every lover's heart knows
being on the path is the ecstasy
spiraling within the jewel.

The moment our lips meet,
our bodies become humble servants
of the beloved,
moving with tides of passion,
activating worlds.

We cultivate union,
breathing through our intimacy
in harmony with celestial spheres,
in the dawn of eternal spring.

The path of love is infinite
because the beloved travels there,
waking poetry in our hearts
and calling us to celebration,
shattering time
and any hope of return.

Our Role

What love will we create
for the earth today?

Trees and stones know,
because they travel all night
among the stars,
going over every detail
of her plan.

First light comes over the ridge,
silhouetting trees
in silver and green.

Birds begin their morning serenade,
letting everyone know
she has arrived.

Flowers catch the sun
and shudder,
as radiance enters their being.

Presences receive instructions
and begin to sway,
singing with expectation
while we wake.

These special realities
manifest to express her love
while we request
the glory of union
with her body of light.

Our hearts catch the sun
and pulse with excitement
at our role
as lovers
in the awakening.

Partner for the Journey

We discover who you are.

Disguises fade with time,
exposing the truth.
Camouflage conceals the treasure
until radiance transforms
those veils as well.

Denial too is temporary,
for you never go away,
always alert for opportunities.

You discover who we are.

When we first met,
we knew immediately
that resistance was useless.
We share our intimacy
in the absolute present,
revealing the jewel.

We are another you,
with body, mind, and soul,
come to be your mirror
and partner for the journey.

The mystery defines the path,
each step traversing the earth
with delight and discovery
as separateness fades away.

Held by a Rainbow

Sneak up on your dream,
entering its reality undetected —

A meadow in majestic mountains
with a cottage near a stream.

Lovers in harmony with the earth,
held by a rainbow.

You and I living a life
of beauty, love, and grace.

Like the Flower

We bring you life,
soaring with the wind
over the surface of your body,
tickling you with kisses.

The universe receives our signal
with each heartbeat
as we dance through the night,
singing to the stars.

A final cleansing transforms us
and alchemy works its magic,
celebrating intimacy
every moment of the day.

The mother holds her child close
to the fire in winter.

The earth holds us in a blue sky,
radiating green abundance
from her heavenly home.

We catch a wave
with our boundless imagination,
giving us wings and vision
to become magnificent,
like the flower
whose pulse is a day.

Spreading Beauty

At the stage of life
when there appears to be a pause
and everything is in balance,
we meet.

Time and space cease
as we enter pure consciousness
with our hearts exposed,
spreading beauty and love
throughout eternity.

Smile and Nod

We grow old in human forms
through many incarnations,
mellowing our intention
and need for perfection.

We no longer seek success and fame,
or place our attention on fear,
abundant in our world;
rather, we tune to the
beloved's celestial harp
and infinite wisdom.

We smile and nod
with everyone coming for council;
our life is a sparkle,
our presence
a catalyst for love.

This death, this birth,
leaves us naked and free —
like a mirror,
empty and innocent.

Missions of Passion

In the land of enchantment
at the hour of forgiveness
we cultivate the earth
and raise our children.

In the arms of love
at the breast of beauty
we resonate with creation,
bringing peace to the land of Eden.

In the splendor of the universe
we dance through the night,
sending stars on missions of passion,
leaving worlds in their wake.

We enter the magnificence,
joining a chorus of lovers
singing to the beloved.

Living the Dream

The dream begins in a meadow,
with you running through
a profusion of flowers,
arms lifted to the sky.

I watch you
from a grassy knoll
in the warmth of the sun,
marveling at your beauty.

The dream has its own viewer,
watching us,
young lovers on a green earth,
expressing the power and simplicity
of innocence.

Color transforms the air,
pulsing from every particle,
emerging, blending,
disappearing in that of the other.

We know the mysteries of nature
and feel the beloved's presence,
understanding the past,
divining the future.

Our bodies carry messages,
absorbing and releasing her fragrance
everywhere we go.

The ecstasy of oneness
covers the earth
and life chants
the beloved's name.

We are the chosen ones,
who walk the earth
telling the saga of love
and living the dream.

Her Most Recent Flowers

The goddess dresses with wonder,
being one with herself.

She beckons us to join
the circle of initiates
in pursuit of truth and wisdom.

She invites our sacred selves
onto the dance floor of life,
spinning in ecstasy.

She enters us
and we forget who we are,
as the language of devotion
consecrates reality.

We meet in meadows of delight,
lovers traversing the web of time,
making music from our goddess souls
and stories for cold winter nights.

Our children
are her most recent flowers,
divulging the source of beauty,
love, and grace.

Setting up Shop

Excitement rises
like a river in spring,
bringing us the message
that near,
very near,
there is a doorway
to unconditional love.

We enter
as judgment turns to compassion
and fear becomes awareness
of the potency.

Closed minds and hearts
turn inside out,
offering myriad possibilities
with courage to seek the treasure.

We live by the river,
setting up shop for pilgrims
moving between worlds at will.

Portal of Initiation

We recognize each other as children,
our hearts open to love
in the innocence
and excitement of life.

Knowing bears the eternal
and our willingness
keeps the fires burning,
warming the earth
with imagination.

We own an assortment of clothes
for many occasions
yet dress in primordial rags
that are thin and transparent.

Our geometry opens a divine matrix,
creating a portal of initiation
for enlightened souls.

We are the wisdom keepers
here to witness the awakening,
remembering the temple of love.

Becoming Light

We stand on a ridge,
a green, lush valley below
and snow-covered mountains above.

We come from the temple of the sun,
in balance with the earth,
bringing our crystal strands
to the temple of the moon.

We sense presences
on all layers of existence,
delivering messages and gifts
from sacred sites
to our relations.

We are ablaze with love,
twin souls called to reunion,
traveling on the breath
of the beloved,
becoming light.

Pool of Shimmering Rubies

We prepare for the best part,
the moment of transformation
that forever opens the way
to the beloved's heart.

Everything turns fuzzy
and hard substances break up,
like a reflection
disturbed by another reality.

Nature speaks,
throwing her arms about us —
a thousand excited voices
in wind and rustling leaves,
telling their secrets to one another
and to us.

We see you for the first time,
virgin and spring,
a fairy
weaving a web of magic,
lover and twin soul
peeling away the veils
at the altar.

The best part has not been written,
the now at the edge of time,
blending realities
in the manifestation of love
with screams of ecstasy
splitting the stars
into a pool
of shimmering rubies.

Wings of Light

In the garden and the city
a profusion of flowers
opens to our love.

We come on wings of light
from one to the other,
gathering sweetness.

Chorus of Mystic Poets

Voices resound in us,
a chorus of mystic poets
singing songs of praise
to the beloved.

She walks in the garden
with flowers bursting into bloom,
calling her children to feast
on divine nectar.

Lovers meet on the path,
entering her spell
with time in suspension,
dancing through the night.

Galaxies are born,
expanding in every direction,
embellishing her voluptuous breasts
with jewels of devotion.

We are like small boats
on an ocean of bliss,
sinking in her depths,
silent and still.

Poetry awakens every day
to speak a new language
expressing the mystery of love.

We recognized each other
on our first meeting,
waiting for the opportunity
to be lovers.

Once Again

The priest
builds temples.

The priestess
makes them sacred.

Perfect union,
once again.

Free Rein

Poetry comes each morning,
rising from the calm,
a reflection in the stillness,
a window to the beloved's heart.

We wake with memories
shining in our eyes,
like a silvery sea.

We clear our active minds,
allowing consciousness free rein
to explore union.

A pebble in the stillness
or a breath from the beloved,
and ripples dance across the surface,
bringing the dream to life.

We become the reflection,
our souls a kaleidoscope,
fashioning elegant masterpieces
shimmering with light.

Single Brilliance

Nothing exists but you!

All pretenses fade
and every game is played out.

What we perceive as dying,
is birth
seen through the eyes of our souls.

What we take for pain,
is waking to the mystery
and ecstasy of your presence.

Longing is your messenger,
reminding us of union
that obliterates existence,
bringing new ways
to see the world.

We give birth to twins
in a garden without walls,
appearing as a single brilliance
on the dance floor of life.

Chamber of Innocence

Even the doorway disappears
when we play together,
and a warm spring surges
from the center of our being.
A knowing fills our minds
with gentle whispers,
I love you.

A fire burns beyond the fire
in our hearth
and that is where we make love,
with flames leaping high,
licking the sky,
consuming mortality with kisses.

We long to become
more and more naked,
to expose the most sensitive places
with the magic of our embrace,
to enter the chamber of innocence
with eyes of passion,
dissolving the past
in love and devotion.

Three of Us

When we feel separation,
longing opens our eyes
to the beauty we seek.

Love comes at every turn,
reminding us
of our passion for life.

Three of us initiate this affair,
love, lover, and beloved,
each the other,
a single existence.

We send the message
This is about love!
Beyond identity, freedom reigns.
Within freedom, there is a bond
with all that is.

The moment consciousness comes
we see truth everywhere,
choosing again and again
to return to this holy shrine.

Sovereignty of Love

Snow holds light in its crystal essence,
presenting a dance floor for shadow,
bringing messages from the beloved
to her children.

She lies on yielding branches
like a lover,
pulling them to earth,
and they return the ecstasy
trembling, reaching for the sky.

Wind arrives on the scene,
loosening the snow
and setting everything in motion,
like kisses activating the stars.

We dream in these bodies
until we wake,
with every fiber of our being
connected to the beloved.

We dance, like shadows
on the floor of life,
seeding the earth with love.

Villages of peace appear
encompassed by a web of protection,
where children,
held in love's arms,
grow strong.

The snow melts
and sweet moisture
enters the receptive earth,
carrying dreams of abundance
to her crystal core,
calling for the sovereignty of love
throughout the cosmos.

Mystical Wheel

The mystical wheel of time turns
as we approach completion.
In the final hour of separation,
we find love.

Wonder replaces memory
and we dream of paradise,
a dream so real
we shall never wake.

We sense presences about us
and our consciousness expands,
revealing the unknown
weaving tapestries of awareness
through the dimensions.

We cross the threshold
to the beloved's chamber
of annihilation and innocence.

She greets us,
holding us close to her heart,
infinite and whole,
spinning in ecstasy.

Our Occupation

Emissaries of love
unfold in the glory of the beloved,
as sound becomes music
and light gives its best part
to our imagination,
birthing poetry and song.

Birds, born of air,
sing to her heartbeat,
and fish keep her pulsing tides
inside their buoyancy.

Words from our morning prayer—
We are one—
resound in our hearts,
and unconditional love
brings consciousness for union.

We live the mystery,
tending the beloved's garden
of green abundance
for our occupation.

Allow the Illusion

In the presence of the beloved
we choose freedom.

In the unfathomable nothingness
we appear transparent,
our souls playing in the garden,
cooing in a magical language.

Voices come to us in constant chatter,
consuming the present with feelings
from a lifetime of enchantment.

We lost our innocence
when we were given a name
and taught a foreign language.

We were born from alchemy
with transformation for our task,
giving us choice and freedom.

We tend her sanctuary with care,
holding each other in the
childhood of existence.

Truth and beauty adorn
the beloved's altar,
making thoughts and sensations
conscious for the first time.

We allow the illusion
with transparency as our guide,
freeing voices of adoration
for the beloved.

Magnificent Mists

We agreed to come together
in the midst of our lives
to build a garden
with ten thousand verses,
uncovering the mystery.

We long to merge,
opening a doorway to beauty
beyond this world
and the magnificent mists
of our passion.

Some part of us remembers
living by the sea
in intimate communion,
weaving tales of wonder
and singing songs of creation.

We carry the myth and legend
passed on for eternity,
with birdsong
echoing in our hearts,
remembering the part
we came to play.

Awakening Ancient Memories

You sing to the beloved
as you walk through her meadows
and shine your green eyes,
like emeralds, into existence.

You touch me with ecstasy,
awakening ancient memories
hidden in my heart,
your lips and breasts on my skin
annihilating sanity.

Passionate and restless,
you enter my reality,
turning hopes and dreams
to myriad images
of paradise.

The mystery lives in us,
completely free,
unbound by love,
laughing like a mountain stream
that knows the ocean intimately.

Final Revolution

Some kind of magic happens here,
with a stream of consciousness
extending through time,
exposed and available.

Human beings cross thresholds
into new worlds,
navigating with love.

Twin souls find each other
and bring passion to earth,
building communities for lovers.

We live the mystery
in bodies of light,
approaching end and beginning
with love and grace.

We slip between the veils
and center our being
on the final revolution —
the alignment of innocence
in our hearts.

Exquisite Silence

Silence speaks first and last,
connecting worlds
with absolute truth.

Our minds create fear and pain
shattering the silence,
and a small being with a big hammer
justifies existence.

Beyond silence,
harmonies focus on the beloved
and we make music
with our hearts and hands.

Songs of victory resound
and the cycle of life continues,
as we seed the earth with love
from her exquisite silence.

Sacred Seeds

We bring seeds of inspiration
from the beloved,
that we received on our way
to join a chorus of lovers
aboard a magic carpet
destined for earth.

Spring announces our arrival
and birds sing about it,
as the sun climbs high
to get a better look
at the birth of love.

Ancestors clean house
for the celebration
and we come through the door
bearing her sacred seeds
that grow ripe from our presence.

We meet in the garden
with excitement and anticipation,
joining hands and hearts,
encompassing existence.

We open the earth like a lover,
experiencing the sensation
and rich fragrance
of the beloved's womb,
planting our dream in darkness
to sprout in the innocence
of a new day.

Becoming Poetry

She is here,
looking for an opening
to our hearts
so she may enter,
becoming poetry.

Dancing Together Again

Creation gathers about the beloved
to ask her what she wants
in the diamond center of her being.

Lovers open the sanctuary
to honor her presence
and channel rainbow light
to human fabrics.

The path accelerates toward
infinite bliss,
birthing our inner sun
with the warm glow of awareness
emerging from our souls.

A council of lovers gathers
in a field of ethereal light
to usher in a cycle of time
with love and compassion.

Language gives birth to song,
resonating with the desire to be free,
exploring the most intimate places
of oneness.

Priest and priestess arrive
surrounded by a matrix of light,
spinning magic for existence.

We invoke her sublime beauty
and her sanctuary becomes a lens
for spirit to kiss the earth.

We sweep the floor of her temple
and bring life to her meadows,
dancing together again.

Speaking the Pain

Sadness bears joy
and seeds for transformation.
Speaking the pain
brings us face-to-face
with the beloved.

Tenacity rules the day
and we ask with our whole being
for divine guidance
while fear guards the gate
to paradise.

Love heals our wounds
and scars liberate stories
we share with friends and lovers.

The unknown has death at the entry,
reminding us that change
is at hand.

Life waits on the other side
and fear creates defenses
with a thousand forms
of avoidance and disguise.

Life consumes death and waits
as we become courageous,
entering the vast unknown.

The beloved holds us in her arms,
knowing the sorrow of separateness
and the ecstasy of unconditional love.

Tasting Nectar

We go from here to there
like butterflies
tasting the nectar of the beloved,
weaving a mantra of light
among the souls we encounter.

Labyrinth of Her Heart

We grow old,
experiencing time through our bodies,
shells of immense beauty
on an ageless beach,
lapped up by the ocean
and ground to sand.

In the ocean we spread out,
absorbed by the pulse,
a thousand voices
within a single being,
singing the poetry of life.

In every verse,
we merge and become separate,
merging again and again.

We grow young,
these bodies becoming eternal
as our souls assimilate beauty,
bringing joy to the beloved
and completing the labyrinth
of her heart.

How could she have known
the gift and sacrifice of love
without our
finding each other in this infinity
of time and space?

Flesh and Bone

We found a place,
peaceful and beautiful,
with spirit to guide us
on the path of light—
this love,
bundled in flesh and bone.

We Say Yes

We say yes
and melt in a sea of splendor,
sacrificing freedom for love.

Why not be a poet
when poetry flows in your blood?

Why not sing
when joy abides in your heart?

Our story speaks of birth,
the journey of preparation
and completion.

We say yes
and the only possibility for oneness
is annihilation of separateness.

Our story speaks of death
until love is a universal language
and our task is complete.

The Tavern

In the tavern everyone looks familiar.
The same ones come and go
for an eternity.

Singers and poets serve wine
from the beloved's heart
and the hall is filled
with laughter.

We appear and disappear
a thousand times
in a single night,
conversing with the stars.

ALCHEMY

Enter here,
the realm of alchemy,
and soar on wings of magic
along the yellow ray of love
with your intuition open
to her spirit.

Celebrating Alchemy

We apprehend the world
with thoughts and feelings
as if we were a point of consciousness
at the center of existence.

Vulnerable and fragile,
we seek sanctuary in the temple
of love and devotion.

We sing in the heavenly choir,
many voices harmonizing earth
in recognition of freedom.

We give unconditionally,
shining like a star
whose light is eternal,
emanating from our breasts.

Through our lovemaking
we turn inside out,
our liberated souls merging,
moving within each other,
celebrating alchemy.

Levity of Love

We live in suspension,
conscious of the mystery
yet able to distinguish
subtle nuances of being—

the beauty of a face
alive with the purity of soul,

wind singing through the trees
like a hand caressing the earth
and soothing her pain,

the beloved
in a matrix of divine light
watching us through our eyes,

sounds and ecstasies
using language and song
for bodies and organs of delight.

We reside in the beloved's heart
like a star
sending light through the universe
and becoming human
to experience the levity of love.

Web of Existence

Enter the realm of magic,
where the mystery is poignant
and the presence of spirit reigns.

Play with divine essence,
moving between worlds at will
with the wand of transformation
and power of creation.

Allow the substance of separateness,
our unique points of view,
to melt and blend
in the beloved's fire.

Feel the womb of the world open,
freeing harbingers of our hearts
to sing songs of love.

Let death come,
knowing that each crossing
unites us with the beloved.

We enter existence
dressed in geometries of light,
exposing beauty wherever we go.

With gestures of control
we veil the beloved;
with conscious action
our wand of truth
sets her free.

Live in joy,
planting seeds
for unconditional love,
weaving realities
for the web of existence.

Light and Love

Love, like light,
unseen and without measure,
illuminates the lover.

The mind creates theories
to explain light's behavior,
while she remains a mystery,
defying definition,
behaving in unpredictable ways.

All being comes from light,
the elemental link to spirit,
the primal substance of creation
taking on form and illuminating herself.

Light and love accentuate existence,
setting stars in the night,
bringing consciousness
and compassion to earth.

The eye embraces objects,
perceiving the nature of substance,
becoming sight
created by light.

The heart embraces the beloved,
perceiving the nature of spirit,
becoming lover
created by love.

We travel in chariots
with organs for love,
sending ecstasy to the cosmos
to become the stars.

Light and love manifest in poetry,
illuminating the beloved,
giving birth to lovers
whose eyes see her everywhere.

Codes of Creation

When we make love
we enter sacred space
and our hearts translate reality
into a symphony of praise.

Thoughts turn to song
and words
to cries of ecstasy
as spirit enters our being.

We appear as rivers,
coming together in celebration of life
to explore her holy chambers.

We dress in poets' garb,
laying a trap for love,
each catch increasing our appetite
until we wake
inside the resonance.

Our kisses produce nectar
that intoxicates lovers
and their dreams carry us
beyond our imagination,
where passion becomes sight.

The mystery is poignant,
like a spring morning,
activating our senses
with joy.

We make love
and a flower opens,
releasing fragrance to the beloved,
who sends us
codes of creation.

Doorways Through the Mist

We slip independently through the mist
to find the chamber of love.

The beloved gives us bodies
and sacrifices her heart
for the gift of praise,
filling the air
with fragrance, music, and light.

A version of reality surrounds us,
where we live in peace,
awakening our souls
to unconditional love.

There are places on earth
where hearts take root,
growing in the garden
of green abundance.

Gemstones permeate the blood
signaling to the cosmos
to weave a web of wonder
around the earth.

We feel the beloved,
her faith and perseverance
knowing the mist will clear
and lovers everywhere
will rivet their attention on her.

We come perfectly matched,
dressed in veils of luminous colors,
playing celestial harps.

When we encounter each other,
our crystal strands resonate,
forming doorways through the mist.

I love you,
the password,
I love you,
the greeting—
and when we meet,
we remember our bliss.

Hymns of Love

Everything around us
appears to be real.

Our senses acknowledge presence,
yet we know that wood rots
and stones wear away,
forming again and again.

Movement is the secret to immortality,
changing with our heartbeats,
serving our intention
for peace, love, and joy.

Everything falls in place
like a sand painting,
made with loving hands,
tossed to the wind
in prayer.

We are that prayer
coming to human form,
beautiful and magnificent
to inspire the world.

We feed the beloved's inspiration,
sending waves of passion
to the cosmos,
vibrating for eternity
as hymns of love.

Poetry and Music

From the heart of the beloved
love pours over the land,
bringing life and sensation,
poetry and music,
to her creatures.

Moment of Ecstasy

The moment love longs for
captures our awareness.

Channels open to the beloved,
rendering a new language
for the earth.

Words manifest in truth,
revealing to the world
possibilities for freedom.

Poetry opens our hearts
sharing the intimacy of union
with every breath and smile.

Artists and bards arrive on the scene,
come to heal pain with beauty
and transform fear
with a song.

Our voices resound in the world,
opening the way to love
as all else fades away.

Imagine the moment
when we become transparent,
exposed to oneness.

Light is all there is,
light shining out of light,
playing within itself,
feeling triumph and joy.

Love is all there is,
love blending with love,
merging in our embrace
in a moment of ecstasy.

Divine Madness

Divine madness rises from our souls
like apparitions on a mountain lake,
close and intimate
in the stillness.

Magic exposes our intention
in every moment,
as we wake for the first time
in each other's arms.

The glow of dawn leaves us
enchanted from the beauty,
light shimmering on the horizon,
spreading across the sky.

Stratums of the beloved
dance on the surface of our bodies
dreaming love in our hearts
and merging with her reality.

We join her in paradise,
pulsing with waves of passion,
entering the night
to discover earth as a star.

Opening into a Flower

A wave rushes to shore,
cleansing our souls
and purifying our hearts,
returning to the ocean.

We herald the beloved,
alerting her to our presence,
as the alchemy of our love
transforms the earth.

This planet of green abundance
resembles a bud,
opening into a flower
in the magnificent garden
of her infinite universe.

We collect the nectar,
giving fragrance and light
to the cosmos
and, sounding a note of ecstasy,
return to the shore.

Turned Inside Out

A sacred council gathers
at the beloved's feet,
seeking guidance and inspiration.

A column of golden light,
woven in exquisite geometry,
defines a ring of being,
activating her matrix
in the earth.

We enter her heart,
our crystal strands glowing,
pulsing with the message
of love and reunion.

Be still and listen
as she speaks with many voices
to our majestic minds.

Be aware of her presence,
past and future,
drawn to our sacred center
and placed in a column of light,
aligning with the stars.

Majesty on every layer of being
sings verses of love,
activating celestial realms,
bringing beauty to the earth.

Our golden sphere
of consciousness
expands to the infinite,
becoming absolute truth
turned inside out.

Dipping into Time

Artists reveal the unknown
on the path of awakening,
stimulating our imagination.

Our bodies create life
and heal themselves
with an intelligence
only the beloved knows.

We enter her sacred chamber
with an eagle's eye on reality,
setting our souls free
to play.

In this union
lies the secret we came to find—
her message pulsing through
every flower in the garden.

We speak words of truth
with elegance
drawn from the beloved's essence,
attracting beauty and grace.

The distinction between us,
the beloved and her lovers,
makes dipping into time
an event worth living for.

Purpose

No words can soothe the pain;
no logic can explain creation,
only a knowing
that purpose
opens like a flower with dawn
and offers itself to the stars
each night.

Love and Light

Love and light
condense from the essence
of the beloved,
entering our being,
warming us into receptivity.

Her special fragrance,
lips turned up in a smile,
eyes sparkling with mischief,
ignite the fire of creation in us.

Light permeates the earth
and opens our awareness
as we merge
in an ocean of bliss,
like stars in a predawn sky.

Love brings us the gifts
of empathy and compassion,
making the mirror transparent.

Whatever enters our luminous spheres
becomes visible,
releasing love and light.

Purified Will

When desperation approaches
and fear knocks at the door,
love dresses for the occasion
with courage for her crown.

Even a single separation
must remain for union,
and these intense emotions
must be deeply felt
for one to speak sublime poetry.

At the threshold of the infinite
our embrace is the final intimacy,
devouring memory and regret
in an ocean of purified will.

Activate the Jewel

A tale of mystery
speaks of our adventure,
where we come to earth
to find the treasure
born from the alchemy
of our souls.

Bards sing their lyrics,
rhythms pulsing through time,
as we enter the excitement
of unconditional love.

Mountains and valleys,
great forests teeming with life,
rivers and oceans,
all chant the beloved's name,
bearing the fiery breath
of transformation.

The loss of innocence
and the quest for the jewel,
form a labyrinth of lives
with integrity in every moment.

The awakening,
beauty like ten thousand suns,
ignites in our hearts,
reaching with arms of light
to embrace the beloved.

Alchemy thrives in every kiss,
as lips of passion activate the jewel
in the beloved's heart.

Infinite Possibilities

Infinite possibilities call,
dancing on the surfaces of our souls
like waves, lapping the shore,
murmur with the ocean's breathing.

Column of Divine Light

Look!
A column of divine light!
O goddess, your beauty
devours our senses.

An intricate web
spun from your essence
links every atom in the universe.

A gathering of souls,
innocent and naked,
forms a circle of power
mixing with reality.

Still the dragon inhabits earth,
destroying her own creation
with fear and rage.

We come to earth to make love
with the dragon,
birthing passion and ecstasy,
partaking in the revolution.

One day all beings will speak
the language of love
and there will be a hush
throughout existence,
a single consciousness
in your infinite heart.

Like Clouds

Angels,
like clouds
swimming in a blue sky,
dance over the earth,
forming a web of protection
for our transformation.

Moment in Time

We enter a moment in time
where everything is transparent,
exposing the miracle of existence.

We are the pivot
as cycles draw to a close
and other forms of love are born.

We die into nothingness
and wake in a sea of splendor,
in bodies of light and passion.

She calls us to communion
and gives us wings
to soar with each other
in the majesty of life.

We come to the threshold of love,
where identity is consumed
by a moment in time.

Flesh and Blood

Poetry uses the language of love
finding words to convey the truth,
drawing substance from the stars.

Light beams,
clothed in silken veils,
weave flesh and blood
about our souls,
giving us these human forms.

Immortal Language

Our adoration embodies harmony
carried on the breath of beauty,
reaching far into the cosmos
to discover the ancient text
and immortal language
of unconditional love.

HUMOR

Enter here,
the realm of humor,
and soar on wings of innocence
along the green ray of love
with your being open
to her presence.

To Perform Like Her

Sometimes we go to our hearts
and ask the minstrels and dancers
what songs they want to perform
for the beloved
today.

Everyone gets excited
and starts tuning their instruments,
as love enters
like a priestess
to reveal the magic.

We are given eyes and hands,
becoming artists and lovers,
transforming raw substance
into pure sensuality
to experience every nuance
of the beloved.

She perceives from the inside,
activating drum and flute,
applauding ecstatically
at our innocent attempts
to perform like her.

Fully Clothed

You are naked
and we come with kisses,
placing them carefully
until you are fully clothed,
elegantly wearing our hearts
like a rose
caressing you with fragrance.

⁓

Savoring Sweetness

In an instant
worlds reveal themselves
and every poem
comes into being.

We live each one,
savoring the sweetness.

Ambush

Have you ever been on a walk
through the garden
and had flowers reach out,
grab your shirt,
pull you to the ground,
and make love to you?

We have!

It happens every day
in the garden
that surrounds our house.

Our best occupation
is being outside
with her breath on our faces
and voices calling us
to her ambush.

Light to Ash

As our souls approach,
the creatures of our minds
become silent and still.

They pick up their instruments
and begin a soft serenade
of recognition.

Soon everyone is dancing
and fire consumes our house.

We turn light to ash,
nourishing earth and sky,
as our souls merge
in cantatas of ecstasy.

A Perfect Setting

Hey, you,
with stars in your eyes!

Look at your admirers,
studying astronomy
for a clue to the mystery
of the universe.

You manifest as a finely cut gem
and we become jewelers,
crafting a perfect setting
to accentuate your beauty.

You come as a nightingale
in the garden of delight
and we take up gardening,
cultivating flowers
while you dress
for an evening performance.

Whatever form you take
we accompany you,
as long as separation exists.

On this playground of life
we find a hundred ways
of being lovers
and in one night
solve the mystery.

The Weird Ones

We are the weird ones
who love the goddess so much
that everywhere we go
she appears,
seeing and speaking
through us.

Birthing the Dawn

The beloved's face
reflects sublime forms of beauty
that are lovers to our eyes,
yet
to see her face
we must be born.

Soon we will take that journey,
but now let longing sing
to our majestic imagination.

We meet in ethereal realms
with the aroma of love
emanating from our passion.

Sun and rain tickle our souls,
creating rainbows for fairies
frolicking with laughter.

We know the beloved
in the ecstasy of our embrace,
with a smile of contentment
telling our dream.

We dance in a meadow,
like leaves aroused by the wind
reach for the sky,
coming to rest in her beauty.

We go there to make love,
remembering the ecstasy
of her face,
birthing the dawn.

What's Next?

It all comes down to this,
this moment,
asking,
What's next?

The First Yes

The first yes always makes you laugh
because it's unexpected,
creeping up and surprising
your playful self.

We look for that special opportunity
when fantasy lingers in your eyes
to provoke a smile

That yes draws you into our arms,
where we share the warmth
of our dreams
and remembrance of love
with bodies of delight.

With the first yes,
you create pristine existence
and we hear that vibration
in our hearts' silent chambers.

When we sanctify our love,
cries of ecstasy extend to the stars,
echoing the first yes.

Drop of Light

Separate, we cannot find our center,
spinning like a lopsided top.

Together, we whistle in the breeze,
chanting the beloved's name.

The earth floats in a pristine sky
like a drop of light
clothed in green and blue.

She keeps her balance,
circling the sun
with friends and lovers
who make up the universe.

We live the fiery breath
of transformation
with equanimity and grace,
turning light into love
until the drop of our being
becomes an ocean.

Our Magic Flute

The songs we know are old,
sung a thousand times in every tavern
along the path of awakening.

We look for the ultimate performance
where we make love on a beach
somewhere in paradise,
invigorating our naked bodies
with wind and sun.

Our eyes sparkle
like a multitude of twinkling stars,
birthing song
from the beloved's lips.

We enter holy communion
playing our magic flute,
bringing music to taverns
throughout existence.

Wondrous One

A lover approaches
the sanctuary of the beloved.

Who are you?
the beloved asks.

I am you, wondrous one,
the lover replies.

How can you speak these words?

I am imperfect,
yet the mirror is whole.

Enter,
so I may kiss
the sweet lips
of my sacred self.

The Ultimate Ecstasy

What happens when illusion
gives in to annihilation?

Will we cease to exist
or experience the ultimate ecstasy?

How will our bodies appear
and what will be our mission?

Is it true that we die alone
into the beloved?

What then,
this promise of union?

From the outside we appear
to be different,
save a sparkle and a smile.

Within we know eternal being
to be one with the beloved,
and while the world may fade
light will endure
and consciousness will be
the ultimate ecstasy.

Fragrance

A raging beauty inside us
beats on the walls to be free.

We wake every day with expectations,
speaking of liberation and magnificence
to attract her attention.

Lovers abound
in the beloved's fairy tale,
seeing beyond appearances
to the heart of glory.

She feels our yearning
and comes to the rescue,
satisfying our desire for freedom
until the garden
brims with fragrance.

In the Garden

Pure reflections of your grace
emanate from our hearts
the beauty we see about us.

Each beat activates a matrix
connecting us with the eternal,
and each pulse within your pulse
intimately unites us with being.

Bridging worlds with beauty,
conscious of our many selves,
placing ash in the earth,
we wake
to possibilities of love—
simple, connected, infinite love.

We proclaim a new age,
where curtain and stage disappear,
truth permeating memory
from the beginning of time.

With love in place
and your sacred parts united,
what will be our task?

As quintessential lovers
we return to your ocean,
and all there is
is love.

We must find a new game to play
in the garden
of wonder and delight.

It's your turn!

You choose!

Bodies of Love

We see you,
a beautiful goddess
sleeping like winter
in a mountain meadow,
dressed in snow.

We travel with you
through the doorway of dreams,
returning fresh and remade.

We exemplify you
as passion draws us
into sacred chambers,
activating
bodies of love.

A Drop from the Sea

I love you,
like an ocean
pouring through your being.

Oh!
Do I overwhelm you?

Then I shall be a tear
kissing your cheek
with a drop from the sea.

Poet and Muse

An old man
with gray beard and long white hair
lives in a grove of tall trees
cradled in the arms
of majestic mountains,
backbone of the earth,
constellation of the heart—
a universe of love.

An old woman
lives on a side of the mountain
with the old man
and they tend a garden
of wonder and delight,
activating earth's crystal core,
sustaining the universe
with hope and compassion.

The man is a poet,
the woman, a muse,
and they dream the beloved
into their chamber of love,
warming her with words of light
and hearts of fire.

Our Joy

The pure white light of being
replenishes us
when the infinite beloved
comes to play.

The spiritual warrior
finds balance with the earth,
nourishing her like a mother.

Our joy and victory
are the gifts we receive
from the cosmic pulse of time.

INDEX OF TITLES

ABOUT THE AUTHOR

NICHOLAS MICHAEL MORROW, born in 1943, spent his childhood in Corpus Christi, Texas, near pristine beaches bordering the Gulf of Mexico, where day and night he listened to its enchanting songs. Inspired, he took up writing at an early age, and by eighteen writing had become his constant companion. Every day he would record his observations and chronicle his passion for nature.

 Over time, Nicholas turned his creative energies to raising a family, homesteading, teaching, architecture, building, and the practical arts. Then at age fifty, he began to write again, with an absorption that opened up new realms of awareness. "It was as if a river of ecstatic poetry had welled up inside me, revealing a presence of 'the beloved' in everything from the vastly infinite to the most personal," he notes.

 Nicholas currently lives with his wife MariAnna Lands, singer and songwriter, and their family on a small sustainable farm in the mountains of northern New Mexico. In addition to writing, he produces and performs devotional poetry.

ABOUT THE ILLUSTRATOR

WILLOW ARLENEA, a celebrated visionary artist, has long been captivated by art, mysticism, and psychology. She earned her bachelor's degree in Fine Arts from Boise State University in Idaho and a master's degree in Transpersonal Psychology from Naropa Institute in Boulder, Colorado. Her career path subsequently took many twists and turns—from public school teaching to watercolor painting, the design of ethnic dance costumes, and the creation of fiber wall hangings, wearable art, masks, and collage jewelry.

More recently, her work with luminescence and archetypal images culminated in a series of paintings for the Tarot of Transformation, a book-and-card set designed to assist diviners in reshaping their lives to resonate with spiritual truths they have uncovered. Several of these images have been adapted to illustrate the poems in Nicholas Michael Morrow's Songs of Love.

Willow lives in Boulder, Colorado, where she continues to give artistic expression to the subtle realms of experience. To learn more about her work, visit http://www.designs bywillow.com.

ORDER FORM

Quantity	Amount
_____ *Songs to the Beloved and Her Lovers* ($19.50)	_____
Sales tax of 7.5% for New Mexico residents	_____
Shipping & handling ($4.00 for first book; $2.00 for each additional book)	_____
TOTAL AMOUNT ENCLOSED	_____

———————— *Quantity discounts available.* ————————

Method of Payment:

❏ Check or money order enclosed (made payable to GAIA
   GROVE PUBLISHING in US funds only)

❏ MasterCard   ❏ VISA

_____   _____

Account Number   *Expiration Date*

Ship to (please print):

Name_____

Address_____

City/State_____

ZIP_____Phone_____

GAIA GROVE
PUBLISHING

PO Box 2888, Ranchos de Taos, NM 87557
phone/fax 505-737-2013 • orders@gaiagrovepublishing.com